THE TAO OF ROBERT

道

ISBN: 978-0-9911596-3-5

Printed in the United States of America

Reunion Press
17664 Greenridge Road
Hidden Valley Lake, CA 95467

Other books by Robert Waldon, PhD, ND

From The Voice Within 1981

Anthology of Love 1986

The Soul's Awakening 1987, 2003, 2014

The Robert Collection 2014

Acknowledgments

This is a purely Spirit-guided work about my personal learning from the workings of Nature.

"TAO", literally translated, means "The Way". It represents the underlying natural order of the universe. When we have forgotten how to be in harmony with life, we can be reminded by observing Nature.

This work existed in words alone for 25 years until December of 2013 when I shared this work with Erika Schoell, who subsequently provide the calligraphy contained in this edition.

Erika A. Schoell was born in Germany and came with her family to the U.S. in 1984. Erika taught private textile art classes for 30 years. Her joy and main interest now is reading and studying about Eastern wisdom, and practicing Asian brush painting and calligraphy.

May this writing inspire and remind you.

Contents

THE TAO OF ROBERT

The
TAO
of
ROBERT

TAO

CHANGE

Change

In times of transformation
Little plans must be laid aside.

You must know
Change without loss
Movement without space
Growth without reaching
Duration without time
Expansion without extension
Creation without effort
Individuation without exclusion

Thus the superior one moves in the world,
Without being moved.
The wise will follow,
Being unaware that they lead.

The wise one,
When walking into darkness,
Carries his own light.
He neither bumps his head nor stumbles.
Shining his light directly on the path
He is unconcerned with where he has been
Or what is around the corner.

KNOWLEDGE

Appreciation

The blind cannot fully appreciate
The beauty of great art.
Neither can those who choose to close their eyes.

The deaf do not receive full benefit
Of a moving symphony.
Neither can those who cover their ears.

Those who would teach
Know to bring truth in a form in which
It can be accepted and embraced
By his selected students.
The people grow in wisdom.

The enlightened one
Knows the truth that he is
And chooses to hold himself forth
In a world where he is reverenced and appreciated.
In this way,
He honors himself.
Those who know him, receive him.
There is great respect for all.
The people grow in love.

COURAGE

No Fear

The statesman,
Using many words when few will do,
Reveals his lack of conviction.
His self-doubt is clear.

The leader,
Using great force and ruling with fear,
Reveals his inner weakness.
He rightly fears his downfall.

The mother,
Holding the child who should walk,
Fosters his dependence.
There is much to overcome.

The enlightened one
Reveals honesty in his simplicity,
Strength in his wisdom,
And love in his freedom.
His willingness is great.
He has nothing to fear.

Truth

The happy heart looks on a happy world.
The heavy heart sees sadness.
Those in love, know love everywhere.

The wise one is aware
That those who see themselves as whole
See truth in him.
Those with inner turmoil and conflict
See his seeming imperfection.

Enlightened ones are so
Because they are,
Not because they are recognized.
They know the truth about themselves
And hold to the truth in others.

TRUTH

Constancy

Like the rising and setting of the sun,
Repetition of that which has great significance
Is not monotonous.

In this way, he comes to know
His power is unlimited,
His love, unrestricted,
His wisdom, unquestionable.
The perfection of his presence is undeniable.

STABILITY

NATURE

Robert Waldon, PhD, ND

Nature

The enlightened one
Lives according to Natural law.
He is fully expressive.

Like the ocean, he gives without sacrifice,
Serving all without discrimination.
He is unlimited.

Like the storm, he is intense in his purpose.
Without becoming fixed in one position
He is free to move on.

Like the river, he flows easily.
Moving around obstacles in his path
He does not struggle.

Like the moon, he knows increase and decrease.
He knows neither gain nor loss.
He is ever the same.

Like the wind, he is playful and spontaneous.
Though he is ever moving and changing,
He is not without power.

Like the star, he is focused.
His light is seen from far off.
There is no restriction.

Knowing

It is difficult in the affairs of men
To embrace a silhouette,
Or to pluck imagined fruit
From the mere shadow of the tree.
And, while one may speak to a statue,
There is little fulfillment
If one seeks meaningful dialogue.

The wise one
Expects neither recognition nor honor,
From even the most receptive of men,
When he has refused to be fully present.
To be known, one must clearly be.

智慧

WISDOM

Unlimited

Limits were designed
To contain what is known.
They create separation.

The Natural way
Is boundless and limitless.
Growth is promoted.
New forms are created.

The wise one knows
There is no separation.
His life and his joy
Is opening to All.

YIELDING

擴大

EXPANSION

Extension

After heavy rains,
When water has extended
And the separating shore reduced,
The people recognize the same lake.

As tides come in
And cover sandy beaches,
It is the same ocean
Though its influence has been extended.

The kingdom, which expands
To embrace surrounding countryside
And bring the people under its protective rule,
Remains the same leadership.

The one of compassion and open heart
Extends himself in personal encounters
And in interactions with the world.
He neither loses himself nor is diminished.
He is wise and he is blessed.
He recognizes that love,
Which ever grows,
Is ever still the same.
It is unlimited.

Respect

The sculptor sees the image
Before putting chisel to stone.
The artist has his vision
Before paint touches his canvas.
The architect draws his plans
Before construction begins.

So, in relationships with men,
Unconditional positive regard
Releases inner beauty.
Perfection is expressed.

尊
敬

RESPECT

Balance

The child stands balanced,
His mother to the left,
His father to the right.
He finds his way in the world.

The scholar teaches.
In his left hand, his scroll.
In his right, his staff.
His students learn Natural truth.

The king is seated.
His counselor to the left,
His general to the right.
He clearly rules his kingdom.

The wise one knows his place.
Receptive to the Will of Heaven,
Unyielding with principles in worldly intercourse,
His strength is unconquerable.

平衡行

BALANCE

Silence

Does hearing define Truth?

The sun still shines
When men close doors and see it not.
In willingness is duration.

Unaware of thunder, rain, clouds or sun,
The Voice speaks Truth
And is silent.

The wise know the Truth in silence.

靜

QUIETNESS

Patience

The master chef
Carefully chooses food to be served.
Rice cooks slowly on a low flame.
Fresh greens, on a high flame,
Need constant stirring to reach perfection.
Each requires its own patient attention.

The master teacher
Carefully chooses his lessons and his students.
Each follows the path his own way.
To achieve transformation
Constant stirring is necessary.

Natural patience yields perfect consistency.

PATIENCE

FOCUS

Focus

The raft supports many
Upon the great water.
The weight, dispersed,
Does not penetrate the surface.

The seeker,
Unafraid to plumb the depths,
Steps from the raft.
The water welcomes him.

The foolish
Scatter themselves widely
And wonder why they do not succeed.

The wise one
Knows the penetrating power of focus.
In his fearlessness
There is success.

和口
詣𣥂

HARMONY

Robert Waldon, PhD, ND

Consistency

The sun rises in the morning
And sets at night.
The seasons change with regularity.
The moon evolves through a pre-determined pattern.
The tides, relentless in their ebb and flow,
Are consistent.

To know and honor such events
Brings man in right relation to the world.
To question or resist, brings discord.
He adapts himself to the flow.

The wise one lives with natural strength.
Consistent and in harmony with Truth.
That which is falsely written in the sand of life
Will wash away and be forgotten.
His teaching will penetrate.
His leadership succeeds.
Natural laws endure.

Completion

It is wise to come to the orchard
When fruit is plentiful.
In this way one is filled.
The foolish remain beyond the bearing season
And are diminished,
Attempting to feast on what is no longer present.

To hire appropriate transportation
To take one to his chosen destination
Is wise.
To remain in the coach once one has arrived
Is foolishness or fear.

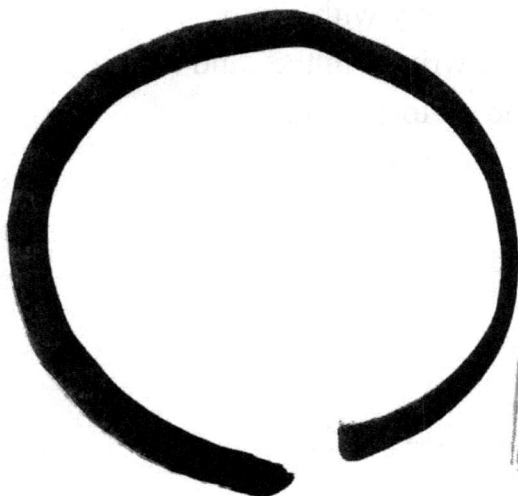

CIRCLE OF ETERNITY

Oneness

The flowing river avoids no opening in its path.
It fully extends itself into that which is presented.
It knows itself in rapids and falls,
In shallowness and depth,
In turbulence and calm.

It is one river.

INNER KNOWLEDGE

GROWTH

Growth

The tiny bird safely develops within the egg.
In nature's way, that bird must break free
Before it can fly.

The caterpillar,
Wrapped in its cocoon,
Transforms within,
Then enters the world
To express its new beauty and grace.

The seed of man, planted in woman's womb,
Grows in its dependent state,
Protected from outer intrusion until it is called forth
To individuate and fully express its gifts in the world.

The wise one knows,
When that which previously nurtured and comforted him
Becomes restrictive,
He must step free and expand
Or he will die.

HONOR

Leadership

The spent blossom drops to make way for the new.

Autumn leaves fall,
When their work is done,
In preparation for Spring growth.

A snake must shed its old skin
So it may fully grow into the new.

An individual must completely strip away old clothing
In order to properly cleanse his body
And do honor to new cloth.

There can be two rulers in the kingdom
Only when it is clear to all
Which is visitor and which reigns.
The old king must abdicate, die or be overthrown
Before the new can be crowned and fully honored.

The wise one serves but one master
For, in truth, that is all he can do.
He recognizes the value in his choice.

Release

The tree does not cling to its leaves in Autumn.
Their falling brings inner strength
And promotes new growth.

Neither does the moon cling to its fullness.

It is the Natural way to empty what is full
And replenish that which has diminished.

A hand filled with stones cannot receive jewels.

EMPTINESS
REALIZATION
TOTALITY

Fear

The frightened rabbit, frozen in his tracks,
Hopes to go unnoticed.

The ostrich hides his head in a hole
And believes he is not seen.

A child covers his eyes,
Certain that his actions render him invisible.

The wise one chooses to look on the world as it is,
Knowing there is no fear except in ignorance.
He knows fearlessness is invulnerability.
How he is seen or not seen is his creation,
Born of a willingness to see all.

CLARITY

Letting Go

Leaves turn and fall in autumn
Having served their purpose.
They are neither collected nor stored,
But left for the wind to disperse,
Then converted into useful soil.

The wise walk always toward the light
Letting shadows fall behind
So they neither darken his path
Nor occlude his vision.

UNDERSTANDING

Flow

Where the riverbank aligns with flowing water
There is peace.
Where the bank intrudes upon the water's path
There is turmoil
And the bank eventually erodes.

By subtle moving in,
Gently caressing the powerful force,
Direction can be changed.
There is no loss in accomplishing the goal.

The wise resist not the flow of life.
They do not invite attack.
Gently holding to their vision,
They create the subtle change,
Unnoticed and unharmed.

江

RIVER

Abundance

The earth gives fruit to be consumed.
Seeds left behind produce new crops.
It gives water to the sky
Which rains in every needed place.
It gives the richness of life,
Receiving power from the sun and energy from the air.
In giving, she opens to receive,
And Natural balance is expressed.

The wise know that giving is all.
Nothing is lost.
Generosity creates abundance.

充裕

ABUNDANCE

Being

The sun shines
Without caring who takes advantage of the light.
The tree bears fruit,
Not planning who to feed, if anyone.
Flowers bloom in spring
Not needing hungry eyes to drink their beauty.
The earth gives life to all who come to her
And know her ways.

A man gives all he has,
Possessions, talent and time,
To those who come into his presence.
He questions not, trusting the Natural call.

The foolish call him crazy.
The wise know him free.

SELF

Yes

Seeds enter the ground.
The earth says "Yes".
Rain comes and sun shines.
The earth says "Yes".
Life is renewed.

Enlightened ones know
To deny nothing and receive all,
Saying "Yes",
Creates a new world.

開懷

OPENNESS

Reflection

The sun shares its reflection in the moon,
Thus bringing Light to a darkened world
Which is temporarily unaware
Of the constant presence of its source.

Enlightened men
Have willingly become mirrors of Heaven
In a world which needs the Light,
Though it may not understand its shining or its source.

HELPFUL PEOPLE

Unseen

Unseen forces motivate the world.

Leaves rustle in unseen wind.
Invisible currents hold soaring wings.
Surrounding air,
Unthought of in its constancy,
Sustains all earthly life.

Unknown forces motivate those unseen
Through true creation.
Like the air, known only by effect.

The wise one lives by forces unseen,
Yet not unknown.
If he stirs the dust of life,
No judgment.

生活

Live

Dressed

When shedding skin,
The snake is most vulnerable
And dangerous to disturb.

To withdraw at such a time serves all,
Until new replaces old
And balance has been restored.

The wise undress in safety,
Going forth to meet the world
Only when fully clothed again.

WISDOM

Death

The Natural way is growth.

The caterpillar does not die
When he withdraws to his cocoon.
The seed does not die
When buried in the earth.
The Sun does not die
When it falls from the sky.

The wise one welcomes the darkness
From which light inevitably comes.
He does not fear death
Knowing it is not true.

What is diminished will be brought to grandeur.

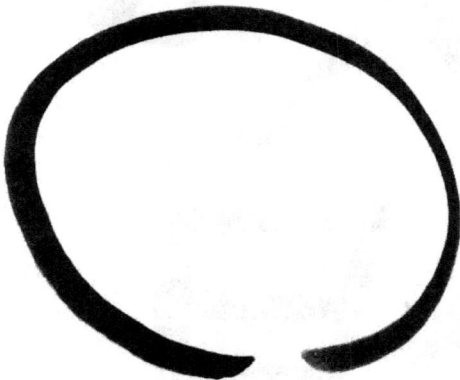

- no beginning -
no end - no

Light

The sun shines when eyes are shut.
Stars still glow when men sleep.
The candle yet burns when placed behind closed doors.

The wise one knows enlightenment
When he wakens to the Light
Which, always, he has been.

ENLIGHTENMENT

Expectations

When peering through a dark glass,
One sees darkness.
A curved glass brings distortion.
No glass brings light.

Believing is seeing.

The wise one knows to expect nothing
And clearly see,
To desire nothing
And be ready to receive all.

PROPRIETY

Self Knowledge

The bird in flight moves with the wind.
When storms abound,
He withdraws to shelter,
Not taunting Nature.

When seasons change
And Summer turns to Fall,
He moves to warmer air
Not needing hunger and cold
To remind him what he clearly knows.

The wise one trusts his knowledge of himself.
Nothing to sustain.
Nothing to prove.

CONSCIOUSNESS

SAGE

Release

Movement long withheld within the earth
Eventually expresses itself in tremors
And the land returns to proper balance.

Energy blocked beneath earth's surface
Creates volcanic opportunities for release.
The land dramatically changes,
Then comes to peace once more.

The flowing river, when clogged,
Will build behind the blockage
Until its power and weight break through
And it resumes its homeward course.

The unaware,
When stopped by fear or outside force,
Notice nothing,
Until the choice for life or death.
For them, great disruption is the resumption of life.
There is no blame.

The one of great awareness
Releases blocks when small
Avoiding the need for cataclysmic change.
Enlightened men withhold nothing,
Knowing their continued flow
Offers no opportunity for obstruction to take hold.
Success is certain.

Wholeness

The freezing wind blows and snow falls
To lie on mountain tops
Until melted by the sun.
The water leaves the mountain,
Some absorbed by thirsty earth
As it flows to lower elevation.
The shining sun warms the lighter drops
And, leaving all impurity behind,
Lifts them to the sky.

To see in part
Is to believe in form and separation.
The water, in its wholeness,
Does not recognize fixation or loss.
It never leaves itself
Or fails to know itself in any form.
Nature's way is flow.

WATER

Peace

The swiftly flowing river lacks depth.
Life within is scarce,
Not easily nurtured in the turmoil.

The great stillness of the ocean is deep.
It knows abundant life.
Its quiet nurtures growth.

In Nature's way, the water must come home.
In this way, the ocean is filled
And each river comes to peace.

PEACE

COMMUNITY

Community

In Nature's way,
The body operates in balance.
The feet to walk,
The hands to hold,
The eye to see.
Each aspect of the whole,
Perfectly expressing,
Without conscious thought, evaluation or comparison,
All joined in common purpose, toward a common goal.
There is great strength in harmonious action.
The body is active, and at peace.

When men gather in community,
They join one body
And each must know and play his Natural part.
Each aspect of the whole,
Perfectly expressing,
Without conscious thought, evaluation or comparison,
All joined in common purpose, toward a common goal.
There is great strength in harmonious action.
The body is active, and at peace.
There is great success.

誠

SINCERITY

Willingness

Salmon swim up stream to spawn
Overcoming oney obstacles and hardships.
In Nature's way,
The committed and strong
Know success and create new life.

The one who crosses the country to attend his teaching
Shows determination and a willingness to learn.
The one who gladly releases
All worldly attachments and possessions,
To receive his highest good,
Shows trust and wisdom.
The one who gives his time and strength to build
Shows strong desire
Which guarantees his own appreciation.

The wise one knows, it is not the distance travelled
Which determines the quality of conviction.
It is the willingness to make the journey.

啓示

AWAKENING

Life

The bird sings
And music is created.
Neither written nor remembered,
It is enjoyed in the moment.

A flower opens
And beauty is manifest.
With no special effort,
The world is lovelier.

The bee moves naturally
From flower to flower.
The butterfly lifts gently in the breeze.
The eagle soars on powerful wings.
One aspect of flight does not limit the other.
It expresses potential.

The wise one knows that his aliveness
Is an awakening to new possibilities,
A beginning, not an end,
Bringing fullness and beauty to the world.

Natural expression is creation, not definition.

Journey

The sun shines
And natural abundance is supported.
The seeker, wanting to know the source,
Eagerly greets the dawn
Then follows the sun's path across the sky
Until it sets.
Then he is still.

The earnest student,
Wanting more,
Seeks the mountain top as closer to the source.
In his climb,
He finds himself.
Reaching his goal,
Yet no closer to the sun,
He knows the radiance within.

In Nature's way, the goal is nothing,
The journey, all.

JOURNEY

Provision

In Nature's way
All are provided for equally.
There is no thought of more for one
And less for another.

Those most closely attuned to the Natural way
Are served with greater care and abundance.
Those ignorant of her ways,
Have less.

The wise one knows
The value of the gift is not in its giving.
True fulfillment lies in the ability to totally receive.

關係

RELATIONSHIPS

Selfish, Picky, Bossy

Vision creates life.
Without knowing the self,
Vision is impossible.
Without living the self,
Its clarity is lost.
Without expanding the self to embrace all,
Its expression is limited.
The selfish,
Knowing their Oneness,
Create abundant life.

Vision creates perfection.
Without a clear desire,
Vision is diluted.
Without demanding all,
Its power is diminished.
Without attention to the smallest detail,
Its beauty fades.
The picky,
Knowing the value of perception,
Create perfect life.

Vision creates manifestation.
Without a strong will,
Vision is wasted.
Without responsibility,
Its potential is unexpressed.
Without a willingness to see it through,
Its service is limited.
The leaders,
Willing to demand the best of all,
Create meaningful life.

It is Nature's way.
Nothing is wasted or lost.
Perfection and abundance are supported.

幻イ象

VISION

RIVER   CHiANG

Fullness

Water poured into an empty vessel
Greatly depletes its source
Before fullness is achieved.
The greater the emptiness,
The greater the danger to the source.

Water poured into a full vessel
Overflows immediately to good cause,
Bringing fullness to those also served
Without depleting the source.
The greater the fullness
The greater the joy to the source
And the greater the good to all.

The wise one
Knows to serve the mighty
And all whom they also touch are served.
To serve the weak
Encourages and supports weakness.

The great lake neither dries up nor empties
Because it is constantly renewed.
Many rivers bring it life.
It is open to fully giving
Because it fully receives.

精通

MASTERY

Moderation

How is it the candle, which is hidden,
Brings illumination?
Or that strength disguised as weakness
Has the force to motivate great change?

The candle sheltered from the wind
Remains lighted,
Guiding the hands which hold it
And available to all when the storm has passed.

The river which moves quietly,
Not challenging men to dam or block its flow
In order to be served,
Moves steadily, unimpeded, to its goal.

The wise one knows
Never to dim his light
And not to hold it forth at the expense of the flame.
He knows neither weakness nor infirmity,
Avoiding needless dissipation of great strength
In meaningless tasks which do not promote his goal.

The blindly excessive promotes extinction.
In moderation is powerful duration.

RESPONSIBILITY

Service

How is it that the little limit the great?
The slow out-pace the swift?
The weak defeat the strong?

The empty cup,
Having a hole at its base,
Can drain the fullest vessel.

The rains do not delay
To give slow farmers time to plant.
Winter does not come late
To protect late-maturing fruit.
The flowing river,
Upon reaching a precipice,
Does not consider the earth below
Before plunging over.

The sun rises,
Even if men still sleep.
Thus, the wise wait for no one
And serve all.

Surrender

The Natural way is choice
And evolutionary change.
All things lead to truth,
Restoring balance and wholeness.

The free man chooses his master
And surrenders to his highest good.
His choice reflects belief.
Surrender brings that truth to him.

For the wise,
Who know holiness within,
Surrender brings life and joy.
For those confused by worldly distortion,
Surrender brings limitation and death,
And a chance to choose again.

SURRENDER

Dr. Robert Waldon, PhD, ND

Naturopathic Doctor

Natural Health Consultant

Specialized Kinesiologist

Ayurvedic Lifestyle Consultant

Touch For Health Instructor

Energetic Life Balancing Instructor

*Minister for Unity Center for Inspired Living
and Reunion Ministries*

Reiki Master Teacher

B.A. in Psychology

Ph.D. in Holistic Health

*Post-graduate degrees in Education,
Business & Finance, Naturopathy, Holistic Health*

Robert Waldon
17664 Greenridge Road
Hidden Valley Lake, CA 95467
Robert@ReunionMinistries.org
(800) 919-2392

www.ingramcontent.com/pod-product-compliance
Lightning Source LLC
Chambersburg PA
CBHW060706030426
42337CB00017B/2775